TABLE OF CONTENTS

For any suggestions,

you can reach us at freedompressteam@gmail.com

Address- FREEDOM PRESS, SCF-32,2ND FLOOR, PHASE–5, Mohali,
Punjab, India Pin-160059
Website – www.freedompress.business.site

A FREEDOM PRESS PUBLICATION

"To gain success, all you need in life is confidence and ignorance"

These two simple words, "confidence and ignorance" if applied correctly in one's life can change the whole attitude of a person. Confidence is the start of success. Until and unless you have the attitude of doing something beyond your expectations, you can't achieve big things in life.

In order to achieve big, you have got to believe in yourself. Self – confidence infuses immense belief in a person thus a person is able to achieve big.

I am quite surprised that myriad of youngsters and students who come to me for studying and counseling are really short of confidence. They lack self-belief and they are not sure that they will be able to get the desired result or not in their lives. This attitude will not let you achieve big in your life. This kind of thinking is a cultivator of failure. I agree that we should not think beyond our limits but let me tell you one thing; only Believers are the Achievers. This simple phenomenon has made people successful, rich and well-known. So, believe in yourself and never sell yourself short.

If this attitude can change the life of the people who gained a lot of success starting from the scratch, then why can't you change yours? Never underestimate the power of yourself. Always think that you can achieve and eventually you will.

- Darshan Singh

ABOUT THE BOOK

This book is not about teaching you how to become a millionaire. Instead this book is a medium to motivate you to take up self-employment or entrepreneurship as a profession rather than restricting yourself to a mere employed person.

I am not against people who do jobs but, in this book, you will find the obvious advantages of beginning a small business over doing a well-paid job. I have very carefully and intentionally used the word small business.

Small business doesn't mean earning small. Business is never measured by the profits that it earns in the initial years, but it is always measured by the value it creates for you and your customers. And the potential that it has for the next few years. Many big giants overtake small companies at a great value because they don't see the things as they are, they see what it can be.

You never judge a business by the profits in a current scenario but the projected profits it can earn over the next few years. If you calculate a new business's profit for the first calendar year, then probably you will never take up a businessperson's path.

Always calculate the gaining of a business for the next 5 years and then judge its true potential. On the contrary, you can never judge a business's true potential until and unless you take it up.

You need to be a businessperson in order to compete on a world stage. There are people who say that business is risky. I don't disagree with them. It is indeed riskier than a job but remember, **only risk takers taste success**.

Without wasting anytime, I am going to take you to this beautiful journey and hope I can influence you that doing a business is better than doing a job in many ways. I will also train you on how to build a brand and carve a niche for yourself.

There are many aspects that need to be covered in order to learn about starting a business. The tips that I will give you is not limited to a certain type of business. You can use this information and apply to most of the products and services that you need to sell. I have used myriad of examples from real life experiences and written in this book for your help and reference.

I am a frequent reader of books. Therefore, I feel that the overall mantra of a book should be understood rather than focusing on every point. Some points given in this book may differ from country to country or culture to culture, but you must understand the crux and apply it to achieve success.

So, let's begin with the journey!

MY BUSINESS STORY

I was raised in a business family, but my father was never interested in roping me or my two brothers in our family business. He had sacrificed a lot and worked day and night in order to establish that business. He always thought that studying was a more powerful weapon than running a business. I followed him and did few jobs in my life but at the later stage I found myself doing business and I was happy, very happy. I started my career working in an electrical company that repaired and manufactured distributions and power transformers. I was an electrical engineer by profession back then in 2008.

I worked for a couple of years in that job and learned a lot about life and how the things fall into place. I earned decent but my desire to go to the next level forced me to leave that job. After that I did job in a retail sector for 6 months, but I quit as there was no growth like most of the other jobs. Although there was less growth in my first job, but I was learning new things every day. But in this job, there was no growth at all, and it was quite a monotonous routine of doing and learning nothing. No learning at all. So, I chose to quit. Then I changed and chopped through 5 other jobs and eventually thought of starting a business. I could have continued any job and would have told myself excuses that I don't know the ABC of business and so on. But this time I was prepared to take the plunge.

I really had no idea how to run a business as I had no previous experience in that field. I started training students for English as I had done a higher diploma in English. I started off with one student and eventually grew into a big brand. I added other products and services that complemented well with my original service. I started my business with a small amount of INR 50,000 ($700 USD approximately). I set up a small office and a classroom. I grew every month and every year. My first month's earning was INR3500. After a couple of months, I earned INR25,000. At that moment, I could see the potential of a business as compared to a job. That day I decided to continue in this field no matter what.

No doubt that businesses are very unpredictable. But that's the beauty of it. You might plan to earn 60,000 in a month and in return you could only earn 10,000. There can be months when you only expected 50,000 but you get three times than that. Predicting success in business can be very trick at the beginning. So, I never knew what to expect from a business.

I will put it in a simple way. I started in 2012 and invested 50,000 in business. My running costs were very less as I had only one staff member and I used to hold the responsibilities of two people. In the first year I earned approximately 100,000. The number rose to 2.5 million rupees in 2017 alone. Is there any mutual fund or investment in property that gives you this sort of a jump? Is there any job where you start at 50,000 per month and dream of ten times raise in 5 years' time? The answer will be no. This can only happen in business. I might have failed and have earned a little amount that year. But that is the beauty of business. in this book I am not only going to tell you about the tricks and tips of running any business but their relative benefits apart from money.

I earn enough to travel new countries every three months, live a luxurious life, do what I like every day, but I think this would have not been possible if I would have stuck with my job. Success is everybody's right. But in this world no one serves you success in your plate. You must earn it; you must snatch it from this world. Your business might not give you the expected returns at times, but it will give you the freedom and peace that is hard to find in a job these days.

NOTE: On most of the pages you will find a line or two in bold font. Those lines are important and have deep meaning. You can write those lines in a diary. By reading those lines you will remember the crux of the chapter easily.

WHAT IS A BUSINESS?

You can find many descriptions of a business in books all over the world. But I would like to keep it simple. **Selling something to make profit is a business**. This whole world revolves around business. Pharmacy sells medicines. Doctors, Attorneys, Speakers, Trainers, Teachers, Mentors, and many professionals sell their advice and skills. Factories sell certain products. Shops sell merchandise. Farmers sell vegetables.

So, any action that involves earning profit by selling a skill set or a product is business. Due to the advent of online business platforms the way of doing business has entirely changed.

Nowadays people are selling food without restaurants. Some people are selling merchandise without having a retail shop or a showroom. Some people are working from India for a boss in USA and getting paid from Canada. Many authors can reach millions of readers and launch their books without getting the books printed. Like you can read this book on Kindle as well. You can get access to this book from any part of the world in seconds.

I remember when the Lock down happened nationwide due to Covid-19, I was able to reach my students and readers through online platforms.

The machinery of doing business has entirely changed from the past but most fundamentals will always remain same. In this book I will discuss the basics related to business along with the changing trends.

If you fail to learn about the changes then you will lag in your progress.

GET RID OF EXCUSES

So, you can't deny the fact that business is a good thing. I hear many people saying that 'you need to lie if you run business. We can't lie so we won't do business. But to me that is just an excuse. It is a fact that most of the people make excuses to avoid certain things. Thus, **people who lack guts will not take up business and will make excuses.**

Another prevalent excuse that you must have heard from many people is that setting up a business requires a considerable amount of money. That is the laziest of excuses that I have ever heard. No doubt that business requires some money to begin with, but you can even start a business at a cost of a smartphone in today's era. But I will explain this at the later stage.

One of my friends was having a healthy discussion with me at the start of 2020. He argued 'I have seen many people fail and lose a great deal of money in business. So, I will never start a business in my life.'

To which I replied and explained "you only seek the examples of people who failed in their business. Look at other people as well. There are thousands of people who became successful after they took up business."

Note: People mostly look for failures, so they are not able to look beyond that. Even if they will start a business, they are bound to fail because in the subconscious mind they were always thinking about the failure's examples. It is important to only take note of positive and successful examples in order to gain success in any field.

WHY BUSINESS?

Imagine yourself working for a company that hired you to earn money for them. You are a part of the chain and work as an important member to earn for the company. You are getting the portion of the company's profit for your work.

The reason I am in favour of doing business over the job is that when you work for someone or in a company you are never given the deserving portion for your hard work. This can be different for some people and for those who earn millions in a month through a job. But most of the people are not in that category. Majority of people earn only enough to run their homes and fulfil the basic requirements. They hardly have enough cash to spend on luxuries and expensive stuff.

I strongly reckon that business is the only way you can get your deserving share. In business if you are not putting in your hard work and efforts then you can never churn profits.

Business can be brutal and chaotic. If you are complacent at any stage, then you can destroy the entire reputation of your business in a matter of days.

Why business? This is not the question for you that needs my answer. I have given my answer above. Now it's time for you to question yourself for a minute whether you really want to start a business or not.

I am writing few situations based on my research. If any of this statement can relate to you then you should leave your job today and start a business.

Situation

1. I think I earn well, but I am not satisfied with 9-5 routine.
2. I can't take the orders of my boss anymore. He's too rude.
3. I work very hard, but I am not able to earn more in the job sector.
4. I earn well, I like my job, but I want more freedom.
5. I don't get long breaks from my job. I like travelling but I am not able to do that.
6. I earn well but I miss many things like spending time with my family and friends.
7. I want to start business, but I don't know the basics of it.

Answer to no. 1 Situation

1. In business you can chose your working hours. You can keep staff to manage the timings when you don't want to work. For example. I shifted my working hours from 10AM-6PM to 7AM – 3PM. This gave me more time in the afternoon and evening to enjoy, relax and for other activities. I like to do work in the first half of the day, so it suited me perfectly. I could do it because I had control over my roster as I am a businessman.
2. There's going to be no boss in your business. Although there would be pressure from the customers to always deliver quality goods and services on time. But that can be managed and if the customer is rude to you then you can always deny your services. If there are a couple of bad customers, then there are millions of good customers as well. You don't serve bad customers. You only cater for the good ones.

3. **Business is the only way you can get great returns for your hard work**. Although there are no assured returns in any business but if you work hard in the right direction then you won't be deprived of success. There is no limit of earnings in business. The more efforts you make, the more you earn.

4. In some jobs people earn very well but are only allowed to operate as they are ordered from their bosses. Creative people will feel awkward in such situation. Business is less about money and more about creativity. If you have a little bit of money and more creativity, then you can certainly earn success in business.

5. Most of the people working in job sectors can't get long holidays every year without strong reasons. I'll give you my example. I am fond of travelling to new countries and spending time there to learn about different cultures and traditions. For that it is important to live there for 3 to 4 weeks. I go for 2 trips every year mostly in August and December and spend a month in a new country every time. I can do this because I have a staff and a team that looks after my work in my absence. This can only happen in business.

NOTE: I couldn't do all of these alluring activities mentioned above for the first 4 or 5 years of my business as there was not much earning and staff to support such hobbies. This will happen with most of the businesses. But from the past 5 or 6 years I have been doing it every year and enjoying my life to the fullest. Growing business takes time. Like a mango tree takes 5 to 6 years to give you fruits. It doesn't mean that you don't earn in the initial years of the business. The thing is that you put the earned money back to the business for the first three years to get more returns.

6. This is the most frequent problem with people in jobs. As I have already told you that I get free in the afternoon and then I spend some time with my daughter in the evening. Also, during my vacations, I go to foreign countries with my friends and family members and spend quality time with them. Again, this is not possible in most of the jobs.

7. If you want to start a business, then the want to start is enough desire to make you successful. It doesn't matter whether you know the basics of anything or not. Everything can be learnt and understood by everyone. Nobody knows anything since birth. All of us learn in this world from people around us and from the disappointment we face with every setback. **There is no such thing as natural talent. Talent is a skill and any skill can be learnt if there is enough want and desire.** Before starting my business, I never thought about the mechanics of it. I just jumped into it and hoped to emerge as a winner. Initially I researched a lot about the business and do's and don'ts of it. Eventually I learned it with experiences. I failed a lot of times but there were small achievements along the way. Those achievements were enough to get me going. And those failure taught me about my mistakes.

I feel that I have given you enough insights into why one should prefer self-employment over a job in this chapter. Now it is crucial to learn the basics and detailing of some other aspects of business. So, let's begin with the next chapter and know more about setting budget for a new business.

WHAT'S MY BUDGET?

The budget entirely depends on your pocket. If you are capable of spending 100,000 at the start of a business, then you can plan accordingly. On the other hand, if you plan to spend a million bucks, then you can make plans differently. **Deciding budgets for business can be very tricky.**

Obviously if you are looking to start a restaurant and you have a million (10 lac rupees) in your pocket then you can divide the costs of equipment, space, staff, advertisements and then proceed in that way.

There is no doubt that to start a restaurant you need to have at least 10 – 15 lac rupees with you. But where most people fail is not the initial stage. Most people fail when they are not able to meet the expenditures with their net income.

For an example, a person earns 100,000 a month from a restaurant, and he/she pays all that money primarily to staff, rent and towards electricity. In that case the income would take some time to increase and, in the meantime, the person may choose to quit.

So, in today's era when competition is at its peak, one needs to cut down the costs. Instead of having four waiters and two cooks. You can have a single waiter plus a manager and two cooks. Surely you can't cut the number of cooks. But you can simply cut waiter's cost and convert into a self-serve restaurant. You don't need an extra person to clean dishes if you have disposable cutlery.

Interestingly **one of my friends started his new restaurant in 50,000 rupees**. You read that right, fifty thousand rupees only. One day he came to me and told me that his new restaurant was getting good response but the rent there was too high. He was only serving lunch and dinner as it was a buffet style restaurant. Moreover, he was getting mind-boggling electricity bills. He came to me because I was the one who encouraged him to open a restaurant as he's a chef by profession and was working with a well-known Hotel chain in New Delhi.

So, I suggested him to open a new subsidiary with different name and do only delivery of food under that name. So, he partnered with a renowned food delivery chain and started that venture too. Now his initial cost was practically zero. He had to only invest in the new name and paid a few bucks to the delivery partner for the advertisement. He roughly spent 50000 on promotion for his new virtual restaurant and got fantastic results within days.

Now in new business, his running costs were literally zero. As he was already paying his staff from the previous restaurant business and this virtual delivery restaurant also started giving him income. So, without extra expenses he carved a new business from the present one.

Not only this, one of my close relatives runs a virtual kitchen. She is a home maker and makes delicious food. I suggested her to tie-up with a leading delivery franchise. So, she simply uploaded a short menu and started receiving orders instantly. She didn't open a restaurant or an outlet. She simply cooked from home kitchen and delivered food to the customers.

In this chapter till now I have discussed about two ideas of starting a restaurant. The first one took 10-15 lacs of investment and the virtual kitchen didn't require investment. Once you start delivering through these platforms then you can gradually grow and expand.

People often make mistake by spending huge sums of money at the beginning of a small or medium scale business. One should start with bare minimum investment and then gradually grow.

There are alternatives and new form of serving customers in every business. At the start of a business if you don't wish to spend a huge amount of money then you must attempt every possible alternative associated with your business and grow organically.

If a person has 100,000 but no creativity, then he can't compete with a person with 10,000 but a lot of creativity and ideas.

Division of Budget

Budget should be divided into few areas

1. Your first small chunk of budget should be allocated towards your brand advertisement at the physical presence. Your physical presence of the shop or office is vital. You must have a flashy hoarding and a logo that is seen by the onlookers. Many people make the mistake of writing too much information than just stating about the business. There should be minimum information on the hoarding and more about the products that you offer. Once you make a name in your business then the name of the organization should be bolder than the products. Because at the end of the day, it is going to be your brand that will attract the repetitive customers.
2. Another 10 percent of the budget goes to the online advertisement. These days you just can't fully rely on the traditional advertising means. You've got to spend most

money of your advertising budget on online advertisement and promotion. Everyone is online in today's time and like to save time by searching everything on the internet. Your online presence is the most crucial factor of your business these days.

3. Now, depending on the type of business you do, 60-70 % should be allocated for the main products that you offer. For example, if you open a restaurant then you spend this money on kitchen and interiors. If you open a coaching institute then you utilize this money for the interior, classrooms, office and amenities. If you open a factory then this money goes into machinery. If you open a shop, then this money goes into the merchandise. This budget also includes all expenses regarding space, initial/advance rent and set-up.

4. Rest of the amount can be kept for running costs. When you start a business, you can miss a lot of running costs in your list that will occur at the beginning stage. So, you should always be prepared for the inevitable. This money will come handy in desperate times.

You can consult a person who's already into business, or you can simply work on your budget by creating a list of items that require investment. Make this list 10 times and every time you make it you will find a new thing, new issue or a new expense. This is how you can minimize any discrepancies in your budget planning.

WHAT'S MY MOTIVE?

It is of utmost importance to ask yourself about the motive behind starting a business.

If you are only in for money, then you are not going to enjoy the other aspects that business brings with it. One of my close friends is a business tycoon and earn millions of rupees every month. I have seen him working day and night from the past 10 years. He doesn't spend time with family and friends. He doesn't go out for vacations. He doesn't even have the time to do his own shopping. His wife does it for him.

I think there is no use of earning that much amount of money if you are not utilizing the benefits of doing a business over job. One day I asked him about his motive behind the hard work that he puts in his work. His candid answer was "earning money". He said, "I like to earn more and more money."

So, his motive was clear. He was in the business only to earn money. But I am training you to take up entrepreneurship for the other benefits as well. The benefits that you will not find in most of the jobs. Don't come into business with a desire to become the richest person in the world. Take up business to become the happiest person of the world who's got enough money for luxuries as well as enough time for the rest of the things as well.

So, before you start a business. Ask yourself the motive behind it. If the motive is only to earn money, then I suggest not to take up business as it will further throw you into misery.

WHAT'S MY PASSION?

Take my word, doing business for only money is not worth it. If you don't enjoy what you do, you will never have job satisfaction. If I like reading and writing books, then that is the job I need to do. But if I am doing something that doesn't interests me then I am bound to fail one day.

If you like travelling, then take up a travelling job. If you like cooking, then don't work in an IT company for God's sake. Don't waste your talent there.

These are the most common mistakes that we make in our lives. I made the same mistake in the early years of my career. But I was lucky enough to take a U-turn quickly.

I would like to give an example here. One of my students has a great rapport with me and he takes my advice every time when he is about to start something. His story is very interesting. He's working in an IT company, but he doesn't like to work there as he's not comfortable with the working environment of jobs.

He desperately wants to get successful. He is single and is above 30 years. But whenever he tries something different, his parents discourage him to do that thing. He is very creative and has tremendous potential in him to do whatever he wants. But the biggest obstacle in his life is his parents.

This is the sad story of many societies all over the world especially in India. In India parents are the ones who decide the fate of their kids. This is absolutely bizarre thinking. This is the reason that many ideas die in the brains of people and are never put to practice.

If anyone demotivates you in your progress to achieve your goal, then he/she is your biggest enemy. No one wants enemies in life. I am not saying that your parents or your spouse is your biggest enemy if he/she stops you from achieving your goal. But they are the enemies of your goal.

So, you never discuss anything with this kind of a person whether he's your father, mother, brother, sister, friend or spouse. Never even ask for a suggestion about your goal/aim from a person who discourages you to pursue them.

If you are passionate enough to pursue a career, then don't take anyone's advice. You will only get confused as different people may have different attitude towards a certain thing.

NOTE: Just follow your passion and don't care what people say or talk about you.

WHAT SHOULD BE MY WORKING HOURS?

Now this is the topic I like to talk about and have changed the perspective of a lot of people in my life. Setting your schedule is the most important factor of a business. This is also the best advantage that a business brings.

Most people have this misconception that a businessperson works for longer hours than a person in a job. They are actually true, and I won't disagree with them. But what they don't know is that it is only true for the first two or three years of the business.

The initial years of a business is the most difficult time and if you go through that tornado, beautiful sunny days are waiting on the other side. That's why most educated people in India prefer jobs as jobs can give instant returns from day one which is not possible in most of the businesses and more secure feeling due to the fixed salary.

But if you take out the first three or perhaps four years of business then I would say that a businessperson has full control over his time schedule, and he/she can manipulate it according to his/her choice and liking. As I told you earlier that I only like to work in the first half of the day, so I only work in the first half of the day. I don't care about what happens after 2 PM. I relax and enjoy the rest of the day. I have so much time to pursue other activities and do whatever I want.

So, it is on you to decide the working hours of your business. Most of the businesses are full time for the first few years as discussed earlier in this chapter. After those initial years you are the King and can decide when to work and when not. If you need a break, then you can put the responsibilities on your staff.

NOTE: Be prepared to work extremely hard for the first few years of your business life. The time will come soon when you will be able to manage your working hours in the way you want.

Many studies have shown that new businesses fail in the first two years because people are not prepared for the efforts and time investment that a business requires initially.

FUND PLANNING AND MANAGEMENT

Fund planning can be very confusing and wrong at times. It is very important to calculate the funds required and proceed accordingly. It is not easy for everyone to accumulate funds at the start of a business.

There are many ways in which you can collect your funds for the business. you can borrow from a friend or relative. You can take a loan from a bank. You can sell your assets. But make sure that most of the money you collect for your business should come from your pocket. That means the loan or borrowed amount should not be more than 40% of the funds you require at the start.

If you are planning to start a business with 100% borrowed money, then there can be great chances of failure. Because businesses don't click instantly. It requires a bit of time and management. But the loan amount needs to be returned in installments from the first month itself.

Again, the fund management differs from business to business. In some businesses you can also get instant returns, but 100% borrowed money should be avoided at all costs. It will only put you under pressure and you might take wrong decisions.

NOTE: If you work under pressure, then your creativity is affected. Creativity is an asset as good as your funds. I had discussed earlier that how creativity as well as funds will help you create a wonderful business. I have seen many people who don't have creativity and burn millions of rupees in businesses.

DIVISION OF COST (INITIAL AND RUNNING)

Running costs of a business are very unpredictable. If you are starting a business for the first time, then you will miscalculate the business cost more often than not.

The initial cost is somewhat easy to calculate. If you are opening a shop then you know the costs of merchandise, advance rent and interiors. A person opening an IT company will know the cost of setting up a new office, cost of gadgets, etc.

On the flip side, it is impossible to calculate the exact running cost of a business. Running costs will depend on the income you generate. It will also depend on the kind of business response you get.

For example, if you are not getting enough response then you will not spend a lot of money on advertisement and miscellaneous things. Whereas you spend money on advertisement and a whole lot of other things if the business is going great.

The initial cost is always high in 99% of the businesses. However, the running cost can vary drastically. You've got to calculate to your best and add 20% to that. That means if you have calculated 100,000 as the running cost then add 20% to that and save it for the first few weeks of the business.

While calculating the initial cost you should sit down calmly and make notes of the things you require. Call multiple vendors and get quotations of the things you need. Always have at least three quotations and then decide from where to buy.

These small savings from initial cost will save you more money for the running cost. It is also important to cut the running costs in the initial days of the business by avoiding unnecessary spendings.

A decent portion of running cost should go to the advertisement. There can be different types of advertisements that will be discussed later in the book. Apart from this, running cost should be spent wisely and carefully.

You don't need to be an expert in calculating the funds required for the business. You just need to make detailed cost sheet and keep on updating it three, four or even five times before starting your business. Every time you will make changes to your fund planning, you will get a better calculation.

START SMALL AND EVENTUALLY GROW

Another mistake that people make before starting a business is that they think that business means earning millions of bucks every day. Business is not only about earning huge sums of money. **Doing business means more freedom**. More freedom in working hours. More freedom in experimenting with services and products. More freedom in everything regarding work.

So, most of the people don't start a business as they think that they need a lot of money for a start-up. This attitude is false and not practical. If you see over the years that most of the successful businesses started from scratch.

That means it is common that most of the business will start small and eventually grow. I am a trainer and I train more than 1000 students every year. I have been in this field for the past 10 years. It wasn't that I got hundreds of students from day 1. I had to work my way up. I had to apply these techniques to my business for gradual growth.

Although I have trained thousands of students, but I started with one. Everything is zero until it starts. And everything whether it is millions or billions, starts with one. You must keep this in mind while doing business, nothing comes easy. No customer is less worthy. Every customer that you serve will contribute to the net pool of your business.

When you start something, it is important to grow gradually. Your business report should always go upward with each passing year. Always make a month wise report of income and customers served. These little things help you find out faults that you might be making. Identify the shortcomings and work on them.

Don't invest all your money at once. Inject your money wisely in business. There can be some ideas that you think will work, but they don't. Whereas there can be ideas that you don't like, but they work well. **It is all about trying and trying until you succeed.**

Small achievements and goals will lead you to bigger success. Set everyday goals. Divide your bigger goals in small tasks. If you intend to earn one million in one year, then it can seem daunting. But if you divide one million in twelve months then monthly target is 80,000, weekly target is 20,000 and daily target is approximately 2,700.

Always breakdown your bigger goals into smaller targets. This way you won't feel the pressure and you can focus on everyday rather than the whole year. Daily targets are easy to manage. Always set a yearly goal but work on daily targets to achieve that bigger goal.

This formula works in achieving everything in life. Imagine you want to learn guitar and don't know the basics of it. At the first day you won't be able to even hold it properly let alone playing tunes on it. After the first day of practice you would think that guitar playing is too difficult, and I can't learn it. Because your goal was to learn guitar but instead of chasing your goal you must have concentrated on the lessons, basics and everyday practice. This way it would have taken you some days or even weeks, but you must have surely achieved your goal.

This happens in business too. Many people give up in the first or second year of the business stating it is not my cup of tea. The first two or three years are crucial. Hence the bigger goal can only be achieved by completing the daily small targets.

It is crucial to start small and learn along the journey. Invest your skill, money, time and every bit of talent you have in achieving your small targets. **Always remember that many smalls make one big.**

INITIAL BURST ONTO SCENE

Once you have decided the factors such as budget, planning, costs and business type, it is important to make your presence felt at the beginning of your business.

Most of the businesses require presence among their customers. These days there are endless mediums through which you can reach your customers. Now you don't wait and watch for the customer to come to you. You must invade their house, their phone and literally their life to make them purchase your services and your products.

The invasion can happen through a lot of mediums. You can advertise in newspapers and radio. But I think with the passage of time this mode of advertisement is becoming outdated. Distributing leaflets and pamphlets is also in the same category. These days people prefer to advertise online which I think is the best way. Targeted advertisement is the best. I will explain about targeted ad in the next few chapters.

Once you are in business then you should never sell yourself short. You should do whatever you can to sell your service and products. **At the beginning of a new business you should advertise wherever it is possible**. Newspapers, magazines, leaflets, social media, web browsers, door to door, malls, at physical locations, wherever it is possible.

At the start of a new business no advertising idea is old. You've got to cover all the corners. This initial advertisement cost should not be part of running costs. It should be an integral part of the initial cost of the business.

I have seen many people investing in making lavish offices or shops, but they fail to attract customers due to lack of advertisement at the start of their business.

You should burst like an atom bomb in your local area as well as the targeted areas. You should advertise heavily in order to get prompt response at the beginning.

A good start is very important for a new business. Try to give exciting offers. Try to keep your margins less and give quality product and service. Be aware of your competitors nearby. Stay one step ahead of them by providing batter quality and rates.

Give better service to your customers. It is rightly said that first impression is the last impression. The first impression that your customer will take from your service will be very difficult to erase from their minds.

Giving good quality products and services to your customers is also a big part of your initial advertisement. They will advertise for you. Repeated customers are an asset and can only be achieved by providing them quality service and product.

You can not last long in business by playing the cheaper cost game for a long term. You will fail soon. High cost doesn't matter for all the customers, quality does.

SOMETHING UNIQUE

When people see your company or your brand, you can't be common. **You've got to be different from others if you want to be successful**. You need to be unique in the way you advertise. You must be smarter than your competition. You've got to find ways in which you can give better picture of you than your competitors. You should stand out than rest of the crowd in many or at least one way. Be it pricing, or the way to present your brand or product. You may use cheaper price of the product or service you provide as a weapon at the beginning of your business. Use this method only at the start for first few weeks. Using it in the longer term can be disadvantage for you. It is only meant to use when you are looking to penetrate in the market.

There are numerous ways to achieve a unique outlook. One of my friends came up with an idea for his business. He was running a coaching center successfully. So, I went up to him to ask about his techniques behind his success despite vigorous competition around him.

He answered with a smile. He said that when he first began, he knew that there was a lot of competition around him in that particular field. So, he had to do something unique. He told me that he advertised for three-day Demo class instead of one day that his competitors offered. He kept the fee same as his competitors but offered extensive study material free of cost. He said that he also offered a week's extra coaching to students. As you can see here that he didn't cut the cost of his product or coaching. Instead offered more to his customers.

To recapitulate, customers are not that concerned about the cost when they have so many options. They are actually more impressed with the ones who can offer them more things at the same cost. Imagine yourself as a customer in a supermarket. If you get sugar for 100 rupee per kilo in most supermarkets and shops, but there's one place that offers 1 kg at 50 and 2 kg at 100. So, will you save that 50 rupees, or you would take double the quantity?

As a smart customer it would be very easy for you to make the decision. Sugar is an essential item and is forever required. You will definitely go for 2 kilos instead of saving 50 rupees as in 100 you are getting double the quantity. It is an essential item and would be required extensively in household. So, buying more at less cost was the best option because you may never get it at such a bargain.

Now let's replace sugar with a broom. Suppose 1 broom is for 100 in supermarket A and supermarket B offers it at 50. It also offers 2 brooms in 100. Indeed, broom is an essential item, but you can afford to save money in this item as the product would last long and you care more about saving some bucks in the present. On the contrary in the case of sugar it was better to take more quantity at a bargain price rather than buying a kilo at less cost.

Similarly, you've got to see that what sort of product you offer and is it an essential requirement of the customer or a luxury one. You will have to play with price and quantity accordingly.

Business is all about common sense and less about assumptions. So, when you launch a product or a service you need to get into customer's shoes and think like them. What you feel best as a customer, you ought to do the same as a provider.

GIFTS AND CELEBRATIONS

It's crucial to keep a small chunk of money for the purpose of gifts and celebrations when you start up a new business. I see many people opening shops, offices and stores but doesn't seem to tell people about themselves at the beginning much. That is a very rude attitude towards your customers.

When you open a firm, you must inform all your relatives, friends and customers nearby. Celebrations doesn't mean spending on food, drinks and catering. It can be simple tea with snacks. It can be a soft opening in which you don't offer party, but you offer exciting discounts and unique products and services.

Celebration doesn't mean eating and distributing gifts to people, it means to let people know that you are in the market. You must be very well prepared for this day and present your company in the best possible way. If a customer or a friend asks you anything about your business or products, then you can't say that it's a new business we don't know much of it. We will tell you later. That is a failure attitude.

This day is your biggest chance to get your first customers. In any startup it is vital to get the first few customers in a short period of time to get going.

So, when you begin, call all your associates, friends, family, potential customers through SMS or by calling them to celebrate the opening and give them small gifts. Give a gift that is not that expensive but very useful. I mostly give wall clocks to my customers and associates around new year. I think this kind of a gift is long kept and always remind your customers about you and your organization.

You can handover useful gifts like pens, diaries or even bags. You can plan this according to your budget, but you can't afford to skip it. **You can't return your first day customers empty handed**. Give them a nice little gift, a cup of tea, some snacks and promise of great product and service.

You and your partner or your staff should be perfectly ready for this day. Dress up in the best possible way (formal). Prepare a small talk or a speech regarding your products and organization. Make sure to be heard by people before they say goodbye. Thank everyone personally who attended your function.

Don't think this opening day as a party day. Think it as an opportunity to impress more people than you will do on usual days. Send invitations to people living nearby through leaflets or invitation cards. Leaflet is a much cheaper option. You can also do that on call or SMS.

You must target the potential customers according to your business type. There can be millions of types of businesses. I don't know what sort of business you are starting. But the basis that I am talking will remain the same. You must make changes to it according to your choice, budget and type of business. As I said earlier business is all about common sense.

I would like to share an interesting example with you all at this stage. One of my clients was running a Traveling agency. He was getting good response, but his advertisement cost was very high. He wanted something organic rather than paid. I suggested him to keep a special offer day in a month at his office where he should invite people via SMS or calls and give his best offers while serving tea and snacks to them to just build a relation.

Now this small exercise didn't cost him much, so he continued it for the whole year. After that time period he felt that he made strong relations with his customers and started getting more leads from the friends and relatives of his existing customers. This exercise builds trust among you and your customers. When your customers start trusting you then they become your spokespersons. They will advertise you everywhere.

Once you serve customers it is important to stay close to them. They are the ones that will help you generate more business. Obviously, you will get more customers from advertisement. But the customers you get from reference are your original customers.

This exercise was not intended to sell his tour package to his original customers. It was only about being in touch with his older customers. It is of prime importance that you stick with your old customers in order to get more inquiries from their relatives or friends.

This is one of the best examples of relation building exercise with your customers. To get more business you should do relation building exercise with your existing customers quite often.

So, giving your customers small gifts and calling them to celebrate small achievements will grow your brand and will expand your business to your existing customer's links as well.

THE HOARDING

Hoarding of your company decides whether you will be able to attract the people near your location or not. Many people don't bother about the hoarding, but it is indeed one of the main parts of your advertisements. It is a free space that you will get for your office or shop where you can advertise freely.

No doubt it should be attractive, but it should be clear as well. If your hoarding is clear enough to tell people about you then you will surely attract many customers from that.

The hoarding should always be colourful and should be in either red or blue colour. Look around you, most of the big brands use red or blue colour for their logos and advertisements. These two colours are dominant and easily recognizable among other colours. I always prefer red colour when I advertise.

These days the market is full of different types of hoarding. The ones with light have more appeal to them. I am going to show you a couple of illustrations through which you can clearly see the comparison and difference in two types of hoardings.

The hoarding in figure. 1 is a poorly planned advertisement. It is unclear and too messy. The information needs to be to the point and straightforward like in figure 2. In hoardings, more focus should be put on the product of yours, your name or brand and your specialty or a unique thing that you offer. There should be no obvious information or anything that is not required in the hoarding.

FIG. 1

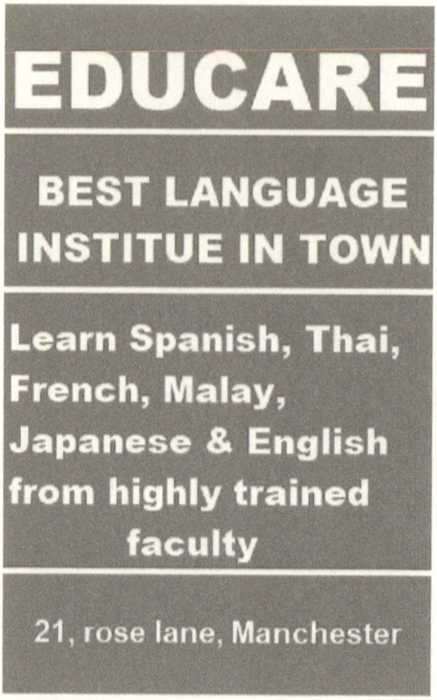

EDUCARE

BEST LANGUAGE INSTITUE IN TOWN

Learn Spanish, Thai, French, Malay, Japanese & English from highly trained faculty

21, rose lane, Manchester

Fig. 2

At my office I always use hoardings that are big and bold. It also depends on the size of the hoarding you are putting up. I use colours from the theme of my office. I am a big fan blue and red colour so I use it everywhere.

BRANDING (LOGO, COLOUR, THEME)

Branding of your name or I should say company's name is one of the most difficult tasks to achieve. Many people spend years and years but are not able to establish a brand name. Selling product is a different thing but making your name a brand is another.

When your name becomes a brand then you are bound to succeed. Branding is a tricky thing and needs to be taken seriously. If you want to take your business to the next level, then branding is must.

Branding simply means when you or your company is recognized by the people through the brand name and not your services or individuals. The first thing that customers must recognize is your brand name and then they will always remember the services and products you offer. Brand name gets famous like a wildfire. But there are certain steps that you need to follow in order to create a brand name for yourself.

The first thing that you've got to remember is that it takes a bit of time. Establishing a brand name isn't a day's job. It requires considerable amount of efforts and patience.

The first thing associated with a brand name is the logo and its colour. Once you decide that which colour is suitable for your logo then that colour becomes the part of your life. That colour should circulate on your website, at your office, in your leaflets, on your logo, in the dress code of your staff, in the gifts you give to your customers, in the furniture of your office, in the quotations you send, literally everywhere. When you have the same colour universally then people start to recognize your logo and colour. Human brains don't remember everything from a single visit. But what they won't forget is the colour. From colour they won't forget the logo and from logo they won't forget your products and services.

Your office theme, your staff's dress theme and every other advertisement should be of the same colour. The logo needs to be simple and easy to understand. Logos that are messy can't be recognized easily. You can hire a professional to get your logo designed.

WEBSITE

The most important online presence for a business is the website. This is where you should not try to cut down your costs. I am not saying that you need to spend huge amounts in the website but never compromise in this regard. You can potentially reach millions of customers worldwide through website. In this era the way of business operations has changed drastically. Now people are searching for literally everything on internet. **If your business or product has a good online presence, then the chances for you to get more customers than your competition is immense.**

Again, your website should have the same colours that your logo has. The website needs to be well tucked at the same time very informative. You must have defined categories at the home page, but those categories should contain a lot of content and images.

Try to add as much images as possible on your website. Make sure to add customer reviews and testimonials at the landing page. Your website should be mobile friendly. Data shows that more than 90% of people browse for products on mobiles rather than PC's or tablets. So, any website you make or any advertisement you do online, should be mobile friendly.

Another important aspect is that your website ought to have an option for your customers to take a survey and ask you questions. This way you can engage customers to spend more time on your website. If they spend more time, then they know more about you. Videos and surveys are the best way to engage customers on your website.

There should be a contact us column where a customer can reach you easily and fill a short form regarding his detail like name, phone number and email id. This data will help you to follow up your customers if they don't show up again.

Website's name should not be long. www.tremendouscomputersindia.com is a poor example. On the contrary, www.tcindia.com is a better one.

You must hire an expert and get the website work done. The content in website should not be written by the website designing company. You've got to use all your knowledge about your business and product, and you must provide the content for your website.

Content provided by you will be fresh and explained in a better way. You are the one to decide the colour theme. Select the right colours and make sure that your content is updated and is without any flaws.

If possible, make some videos and post it on the website. The video should contain the details about the product you offer and the quality you assure of giving.

In my website I have useful content and informational videos for customers to see. This way they spend more time on my website and I get more of their time to allure them to my products and services. You should try everything to engage your customers.

Always remember that website is the main identity of your business on internet.

STAFF

You should never compromise in selecting your staff. Try to keep staff that lives nearby. The person will be accustomed to people of that area. Hence will be better equipped to handle customers.

When you call candidates for interview make sure that scores in academic certificates doesn't matter. A person with more sense and attractive smile or better communication skill is much more valuable than a person with high academic grades.

While selecting your staff, keep in mind that young aged and freshers will learn better and work at a lower salary than an experienced candidate. But you've got to have a skill to teach them otherwise startups and inexperienced staff can be a recipe of disaster.

At the start of a new business you should be prepared to cut on your running costs. You as the head of the business should work as an all-rounder. You must take up responsibilities of two staff members on your own. Instead of keeping an extra staff person, you should fulfil their roles.

Other roles should be wisely divided to the staff members. You must have good camaraderie with your staff. Never treat any of your staff member with anger and use foul language with them. They are the ones who are supporting you in your business. Their wellbeing must be your top priority.

I often do a small get together with my staff every month. I take them to a restaurant and have lunch there. This increases harmony and understanding between us. This really helps us at work. It increases teamwork capabilities and efficiency of the staff.

Never force any of your staff members for over time. Always take out time and hear out any ideas that they have to offer. There can be amazing ideas that we can get from people at work.

Before taking any important decision for your company, consult all your staff members in a meeting. This makes them feel more important and responsible. Moreover, don't cut salary for a couple of extra holidays. Always keep your staff happy.

SOCIAL MEDIA PRESENCE

No one can deny the fact that the social media presence for any type of business has become a common playground for businesses around the world. Again, the question is that how to make your presence felt? You can start any type of business, there will be hundreds of more like yours on the social media attracting the customers already.

How can you be different then? The answer to this question is that **you must have a continuous presence in the social media**. Advertise every day. Make your customers see you every day through photos, videos and information that you post on these social media sites.

There are around 6 or 7 prominent social media sites where millions of people spend time every day. In order to attract the traffic, you must sell things differently. As discussed in the earlier chapter BEING UNIQUE, you need to think out of the box and give offers that no one is offering.

It is important to post information on all the famous social media sites. Post colourful photos regarding your business, videos describing your business, videos of satisfied customers and everything that will attract new customers.

Brain hammering is what you need on social media. Keep on chasing your customers until they give up on you. Social networking sites are a great medium where you can reach a lot of customers through your relatives and friends and paid promotions in a very normal budget. It is about the content you write, photos and videos you post.

These days all age group people are present on the social networking. You find people over the age of 70 swiftly using mobile phones. You can find all types of customers on social networking sites. You can easily find customers for targeted marketing there.

Social media advertisement is a very vast subject. It would require a whole book to write all the aspects. But there's no need of you to become an expert in this field.

You can follow simple steps on these sites while promoting a particular product and you can learn everything from the instructions given. You can also hire a professional or marketing team for the same.

Your primary focus should be on the customers that comes to you. Making a list of your customers and following up them when required. Advertisement is one part of the business. But dealing with them is another and quite a different forte.

You should be more equipped in dealing with customers as that is when you get all the repeated customers and grow your business. Only advertise when you can cater for your customer's needs. Sometimes people advertise heavily but are unable to handle the customers and their demands.

You've got to analyze the fact that your products are not meant for people who are less prone to use social media. In that case, spending money on social media is not a great option.

One of my friends is a dietician and gets a wide range of customers. He is very regular in posting short videos regarding the foods that are good for health and foods that should be avoided. The day he started making videos, he got great response. He posts these videos on all the social media platforms.

His business escalated rapidly by posting videos and he told me about the benefits he reaps from the social networking websites. This method of advertising has become prominent and easy way to get customers. People all over the world are using these sites as their marketing place.

The field of social media advertising is not that difficult, and I remember that I learned it in a month from a local institute and became quite good at it. When I was new in my business, I did all the social media promotions myself and got great results.

So, if you plan to not spend extra money on hiring a PR agency for you then you can surely learn this type of advertisement in a relatively short period of time and do it yourself.

PHYSICAL PRESENCE

Physical presence is equally important as having a social media presence. If you are in a prominent area, then it is easy to have a presence there among a lot of customers. This becomes difficult and tricky if you are in a place that is secluded or a bit out of the town.

Now these things shouldn't worry you at all. If you have the right sort of attitude and planning, then you can have your presence felt in any type of area. At my office I use bold and big hoardings to make my presence felt.

I spend a considerable amount every year on hoardings. The moment I feel that the hoardings are getting dull or old, I change them immediately. Moreover, I use colourful signage and maintain good relations with my professional neighbours.

Always meet your professional neighbours and tell them about what you do and what you have achieved. People in the market can be of great help. Once they come to know about you then they will speak for you and about your company to other people. Often invite your professional neighbours to your office and chat over tea.

Physical presence is not that difficult to achieve but to have that presence you can't just sit in your office and hope to create one. You need to get out, talk to the people in nearby offices, meet them, put large and attractive hoardings. Always participate in one or two social activities every month. This increases your circle. Hence it will help you increase your business.

You must become the talk of the town. This is how you will spread your word through people. People will talk about your organization, products and services. Make people advertise about you.

PR skill is very important in running a successful business. Personal relation skill will help you in every situation. People with good PR skills often succeed in business. There are many ways to develop that skill. The most simple and best way is to just meet more and more people and develop professional friendship.

This friendship should be based on give and take. It should go a long way. It should not be meant only to get help but also to help others when they need it. Slowly over the years these friendships will be like your family and part of your life. They will bail you out of troubles when needed.

Another way to establish physical presence is by placing canopies with advertisements near the office or just outside the complex. If you have good relations with your professional neighbours then they won't deny you the permission of placing the canopy in the market. This is a great way to attract passerby's and create physical presence.

One of my friends did a great job in creating a physical presence for his business. His shop was not located in the center of the town, so he had to think out of the box to create his physical presence. He took permissions from the local authorities to hoist a massive air balloon at the top of his shop building in order to advertise.

He sells sports goods and needed more customer footfall. His idea clicked and he received a huge increase in the customer base after he took this initiative. One day I went to see him and noticed that the balloon was visible from more than a couple of kilometers from his shop from all the directions.

It was a huge yellow colour balloon with glossy look and text written in red: SPORTS GOODS. Such a simple text yet generating great business. He didn't do it for long. Only for a few months and soon his customers became his true physical presence. He was getting repeated customers and a lot of references from them due to his balloon advertisement.

It is important to burst on to the scene initially. If you do so, you can get a head start to your start-up. I'm not saying that you don't need to advertise afterwards. But the intensity should be very high at the start.

You can try your own methods that can work according to your area and business type. What important is that you do something and not sit idle and wait for customers to come to you. You need to get up, try different ideas and see what works for you. The keep on applying those methods to increase your initial customer base.

FAMILY / FRIENDS HELP

How can we forget friends in any aspect of life? Family and friends are the most integral part of most people's life. I have a lot of friends and relatives who have contributed in my business over the past few years. They've been instrumental in spreading the horizon of my business.

I hope that you must have some people in your life who will support to your core. You can take help of your family and friends in getting a head start to your business. You can ask them to share your posts, business, ideas, products and services.

Imagine if you have 100 friends and relatives and your friends and relatives have 100 people each in their contact. Then this instantly multiplies into 10,000. Your product or business could reach an organic growth of 10,000 people in couple of days. This chain will go on even if 10% of your friend's friends chose to tell other people. You must do this at the start of your business. **Taking help from your friends, relatives and from their friends and relatives, will surely boost your business.**

Your friends and family members can also help you by giving you contact details of their friends and family relatives for SMS promotions and calling data. You should never feel shy in taking help from them. Afterall friends and family are the ones who are always there when needed.

I remember when I started my coaching institute in 2012. I told all my friends and relatives by calling them personally and inviting them to the inauguration function. I had some rituals done that day along with a decent party after that. This gave a direction to my business from day 1.

There is no doubt that I had to spend huge bucks in advertising my business and to create a physical presence but the help from my family members and friends was of huge importance. They advertised me and my business without having me spend even a penny.

I didn't spend anything but got great number of references from them. Even today, around 30% of the customers I receive are from my friends and family member's reference. This is a great number as I don't have to spend anything for this 30% customer base that I receive every month. And it only happened because I told them about my business and products. These days people are so busy that you need to remind them again and again about you and your business. It is same for your customers as well. Advertisement will only work when it is done consistently.

When you serve the referred customers and they feel satisfied from your products and services then they become your extended family. Then you start getting reference from the extended family members as well. If you strive for quality and improved service for the first few years of your business, then your growth will be inevitable.

So, it would not be wrong to say that if you have a large friend and family circle then there are more chance for you to grab extra customers through them. As a businessperson, if you can earn at the initial stage then it is nothing short of a wonder.

I would like to give you another example of my friend who is a prominent Youtuber. She started her channel as a food vlogger. She wasn't getting much response at the start. So, I suggested her to apply this formula to her vlog channel.

I told her to share her channel and videos with friends and family members. She had a big enough friend circle and I also helped her by sharing her videos with my near and dear ones. After a couple of weeks, she started getting more views and likes to her videos. That process really worked wonderfully for her. Once she got to 5000-6000 people, she started getting more and more viewers from her extended family and friends. This is how many businesses grow and this is how yours can grow too.

I like images and graphs to explain things. I feel that images stuck in the mind for longer than texts. So, here is an image summarizing the whole chapter:

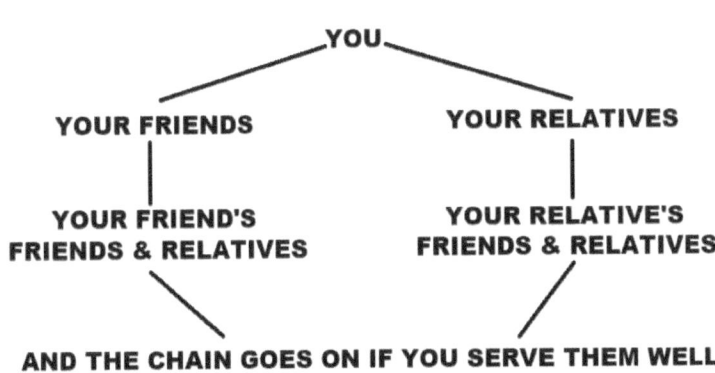

YOU GET CUSTOMERS FROM:

YOU

YOUR FRIENDS

YOUR RELATIVES

YOUR FRIEND'S FRIENDS & RELATIVES

YOUR RELATIVE'S FRIENDS & RELATIVES

AND THE CHAIN GOES ON IF YOU SERVE THEM WELL

EMAIL LIST

Not many businesspersons are big fans of creating a detailed email list of their clients and customers. I believe that it is as important as phone numbers. Though you can reach your customers directly and more precisely on phone, but you reach customers holistically and in detail through emails.

Never forget to take your customer's email id and save it to your list. You can use this list to inform your customers about your products and services. You can remind them about any events that you are organizing. You can invite your customers for a small function through emails.

Emails are more impactful that sending messages on phone. Previously not many people were interested in checking their emails regularly. However, these days everyone has a smart phone in their pockets, and they receive an email notification as promptly as an SMS or any sort of message.

Emails are more impactful and can contain a lot of detailed information with beautiful presentation. You can attach photos, videos, documents, pdf files and much more as per your choice. An email can contain loads of information and important material.

You should send emails regularly to your customers. You must have a signature beginning and ending to the email so that the receiver should remember you from your distinct style of email. Never send emails with brief material as emails are made for detailed information. Try to send photos and videos of your satisfied customers as well.

The reason I am focusing so much on the email list is that first of all it is a free medium through which you can reach your targeted customers. Plus, you just need to make a small effort in drafting one email and then open your list and at the click of one button you can send that email to thousands of people.

Now you might think that it's one of the most common ways that a lot of people apply. But take my word, it is also one of the most effective ways as well. The reason some people are not able to get anything out of this exercise is non persistence. Once you start sending the emails then don't think that you will reap fruits in a couple of months. You need to brain hammer your customers and you've got to stick with this method for at least a year to start seeing the advantages that it brings.

Another important aspect is that you should set a timeline and follow that. If you send your second email after 7 days, then the third should be sent after 14 and fourth after 21 days. Or simply fix a day, i.e Saturday. Your customers should know when they are going to receive the email from your side. They shouldn't be surprised, or you shouldn't send emails on random days. This will not appeal people to see your emails regularly. If they know that they are going to receive an email from your side on a particular day, then they can make themselves available to read your email. They will be prepared to read what you send them, just like an online subscription.

Apart from this, **you should assign a staff member to revert to the replies or any queries you get on emails**. If you fail to reply to the emails, then people will not take interest in asking you questions the next time. You must make people ask you questions. This means they are interested in your products or services. If a customer is intending to spend money in buying a product or service from you then he/she has the full right to ask you questions. Emails are the best way to reply to your customer's queries.

Today if you are unable to convince your customer then tomorrow, he/she has millions of other options. The internet has made things available to people at the comfort of their home. It is a boon and can be bane as well if you don't respond on time.

When you respond to emails then people feel important. They think that you are interested to hear them and their demands. There will be some customers that will be rude or harsh to you. As a service provider, under no circumstance you should engage yourself in a banter with your customer. Losing one customer could mean losing 50 or 100 customers. Few bad reviews can cost you a chunk of your business. For a businessperson, customer is the most important thing. Therefore, respecting them and bearing their tantrums is a part of business.

CONSTANT FOLLOW-UP

When a customer calls you then it means that he/she is interested in your product. There can be no one in today's world who's got enough time to waste in inquiring about a random product. So, when you get a query on email, phone, SMS or any other medium then make sure that you save his/her contact detail.

If you are not able to make your customer's doubts clear, then call them again and get all their details and add them in your list of your customers. Constant follow-up is crucial if you don't want to lose your customers. The competition is fierce these days and options are available in abundance. So, if you don't want to lose your customers then you need to stay in regular contact with them.

Keep on informing your customers about your products and services through SMS, phone, emails and all the other sources you have until you get an answer. If the customer is not interested, then he/she will simply tell you. If this is the case, then there is no point in following-up that person. However, you should not take them out of your list instead move them to another list known as not-interested customers. In that list you don't follow them up regularly but keep them informed of anything important happening or any seminar that you are conducting or any new product you are launching.

This customer data that you collect will be of use to you for many years to come. This data will also let you know that how many customers you receive and how many people buy your product. Constant follow up is not an easy thing to do. You might find people get annoyed by your calls and some won't pick for that matter. You must be very creative in managing the customer data that you have. You can use a lot of ways through which your customers don't feel irritated. Don't shove your product in your customer's throat. Be selective and smooth in your approach. Follow up doesn't mean that you grab the customer by the scuff of the neck. Follow up means that you don't let the customers drift away. Always have a margin of cost in your product as some people can be price conscious. You can reduce price by a bit in pursuit to allure the customer to buy your product.

When you follow up the customer then never talk about your cost of the product or service. Always focus on quality and only quality. Do more research about you competitors and try to give customers a little bit more than your competition. Give your customers at least one attractive aspect of your product or service. **You never play with price; always play with the uniqueness of your product or service.** If you can't be unique then it is very difficult for you to establish yourself in the market.

Never disturb your customers on the weekdays when they are busy in their work. I am a firm believer of advertising on the weekends. These days most people are in jovial mood and won't mind a couple of companies calling to sell their products. Always follow up customers on Saturday or Sunday. Chose morning as the calling time. Sometimes you are selling such products and services in which you must follow up the customers on any day of the week then you should keep one thing in mind. If you call your customers on the weekdays, then call them after 6 PM. No one is interested to take calls while working. When you call a customer the first thing you ask them: is this the right time to call? If yes, then go ahead and if not then politely ask the customer to let you know about the time to call them.

Then strictly follow that time and call your customers. Following up looks like an easy job but mind you it is one of the most tiring jobs and most valuable job for your business. **You must select a calm and cool person for follow up job.** I always prefer a female candidate for this type of a position as they are more patient and convincing. You ought to select the right person for this sort of a job otherwise you will not be able to compel your customers into buying your product.

While selecting an applicant for this job you must consider a candidate who has good selling skills as following up customers is a vital part of your business. Remember that this type of skill can't be taught easily. This is a natural skill that only few people have. So always select candidate with right sort of attitude for this responsibility.

ANNUAL GIFTS

This is one of things about business that I like the most. I have many friends of mine who are in business, so I receive a lot of gifts in November and December. I do the same activity around new year. I order corporate gifts every year to please my clients and customers. **Never compromise on the gifts that you give**. Chose the best quality and gift them personally to your customers and clients.

Chose gifts like customized pens, wall clocks, wall paintings, office table accessories, fancy table calendars, table clocks and so on. These kinds of gifts remind your clients about you every day when they use them. These are everyday used items. Everyone likes receiving gifts. They will be very happy while getting these useful items.

You must have your company's logo and main service, or product embossed on the gift so that it is not only limited to your clients but everyone who sees it. This is a very useful exercise and is working for me ever since I start giving gifts. I love to present gifts to my customers. I have heard from my clients that my gifts are very useful to them. They really like it and use it in daily lives. It has become my habit now. Even if I am gifting someone on his/her birthday I chose gifts that are used in daily lives.

Call everyone whom you have presented the gift after a week. Ask them about your gift. Ask them how they felt about it. In a way you must keep on reminding them about you every time, again and again.

You take an example of big soft drink brands. They are selling their colas for more than 60 or 70 years. They are all over the world with their products. Most of the people drink their products or at least know about it. Even if they don't advertise for a couple of years, their sales won't be affected that much. But they continuously advertise their products. There are two reasons behind that. **The first one is that they want to hammer the brain of their customers again and again so that their product becomes a part of their customer's life.** Second reason is that they don't want any competition to enter the field. They want to be the only brand of that product.

So, from these huge brands we can learn a lot. We can absorb what they bring in the market. Giving gifts, calling your customers and clients is an exercise for hammering their brains. You don't want any other company to reach your customer's ears and eyes. You can't stop your competition to enter the market or to reach the people, but you can maintain a strong impression of your company and brand on your customer's mind.

FORM DEPARTMENTS

When you start growing after a year or two, it becomes crucial to hire more people to grow your business. At the initial stage of the business, you've got to work tirelessly for 7 days a week. You must take responsibilities of two or three people yourself. But once you start getting more response, then you need more staff to grow.

I have often seen people having substantial numbers in staff, but the efficiency is not there. Sometimes restaurants with more waiters are not efficient in their services as compared to some restaurants with small number of staff. This happens because restaurants with lesser staff has managed their employees well and given each member more responsibility to provide service.

When your company grows, make departments so that different employees have different responsibilities. Your job then becomes to manage your staff and listen to their requirements and suggestions. You are then accountable to give your staff targets and analyze them at the end of each month. It becomes your responsibility to monitor your employee's satisfaction, efficiency, growth and issues.

Make sure that every employee of your company is doing well and is satisfied with his/her job. Make sure that the targets that you are giving them are realistic. Make sure that they stay motivated and inspired.

It is of great importance to form departments in your company. This not only increases your employee's efficiency but also helps you to build your product and business.

CLIENT FEEDBACK

This is an integral part for the growth of a business. For me it is the most important part. For others it could be less important. It depends on person to person. **If someone is paying me for a product or service, then my aim is to see the satisfaction of the customer or client**. The customer should receive quality at the first place. If you fail to deliver quality due to some issue, then I feel that you should be prompt in handling their issues and discrepancies from your side. Always accept a mistake immediately if happened from your side and quickly try to eradicate the customer's issues.

I have seen many companies selling their products and not interested in client feedback. Those companies can perform well for the first two or three years, but this kind of approach is not good for the long-term business.

One of my friends was selling bags. He had hired a big store in a mall and was doing well from the start. He mainly sold ladies purse and bags. He sourced his products from a nearby factory. He was purchasing his goods only from a single place. He started receiving many complaints from the customers, but he kept ignoring the complaints and behaved rudely with his customers. I met him one day and he told me about all this.

I suggested him to replace the products of the customers immediately and start purchasing from a new factory or vendor. But he argued that his products were selling like a hot cake and he didn't see the need of changing the source and replacing products of the customers. I warned him but he was in no mood to listen to me. Steadily his product faced criticism from thousands of people and soon became the talk of the town in a negative way.

His sales dropped sharply, and he couldn't recover from that jolt. After that he changed his vendor and advertised heavily for the products again, but people had lost faith in his products. The new products were better, but the company's reputation had gone for a toss. Finally, he had to shut down his shop and look for something else.

Let's closely analyses why his new products didn't sell as he would have expected. **It is very hard to retain the faith of your customers once you lose them. There are other people looking to take over as soon as you make mistakes.** Even if he started selling better products, his reputation proved to be too harsh on him. All he needed to do was listen to the customer's feedback patiently and solve those issues.

Customers these days are more interested in the quality of a product and service rather than the cost. They also expect good after sales service and assistance. Some clients won't even call you and tell that your product was not good. They simply tell people and do negative advertisement of your product. So, what is the solution?

The remedy is that when you serve a customer you should call them and ask for their feedback. You can ask them about the service and product. You can ask them about any improvement needed in that. You may ask them whether they require more from you. You should care for your customers and make them feel that you are always there when they need most.

Remember it should not be a mere formality. If you genuinely believe in helping your customers, then you must solve their issues immediately. If nothing can be done, then simply replace the product or give refund for the service. Because when you design your product then you must be confident enough about its quality. But there's an old saying that you can't please everyone.

So, there will be customers who will not be happy and who would have confusions or doubts about your service or product. Your duty during client feedback is to solve customers' queries and give them a better solution for their problems.

When you call a customer then your main aim should be to find a definite answer. Whether your customer is happy or not. There can be no midway. If the customer is hesitant in answering, then you've got to make them answer in the feedback exercise.

Always remember that client feedback will always remain the most important aspect behind the growth of your business.

PRODUCT ENHANCEMENT / R & D

Another cog in the wheel of growing a business is Product Enhancement and R & D. This is directly linked with client feedback. R & D stands for research and development whereas product enhancement means improving the product. In one-way R&D is also about researching about the product and developing it for future.

When you are doing business, your one set of focus should always be on product or service enhancement. If you don't focus on this, you might sell good for a couple of years but there will be saturation in your sales after that if you don't develop your product or enhance your service.

With ever changing technology, the products need to be improved regularly. R & D works in every field of business. You could be selling anything; R & D is must. **You must be involved in improving your services and products all the time**. It is a continuous part of the business. It is about working continuously behind the scenes to improve the product even if your sales are going up.

Always involve yourself in thinking that what better things you can offer to your customers. When you think about something deeply then answers start coming from within. You should never let your customers tell you about improvements in service or products. You should be one step ahead of everyone and make improvements every now and then.

It should be you who should tell the customers that we have made improvements in this and improvements in that. When it comes to my business, I am deeply involved in enhancing my products. I always think that how I can serve better. Afterall your satisfied customers are going to bring you repetitive business.

There should be a proper allocated small chunk of your initial as well as running costs that should go in R & D. To some people, this might seem to be a waste of money. To others it is improving your current product and services. There can be times when you are not able to make improvements, but you've got to be patient. One day you will find the missing blocks and fit them at the designated place. For that you need to be involved in product enhancement continuously.

R & D will never let you down because when you are looking for better alternatives and improvements then you are bound to find something much better and efficient. My mentor always used to tell me that when you write a plan it will look like a perfect one. Then you write it again, it will seem better than the first one. You write it again, there will be more improvements. R & D works exactly like that. You have a product and you are continuously working on enhancing that. Day by day you will find a small element that can better your product or service.

This works both ways. R & D is always for your betterment. Not only it will benefit the customer with enhanced product, it will also give you more confidence in selling your product. The benefits that come from product enhancement are long term, and they are sure.

PLAN EVERYDAY

If your business hours are 9 AM – 6 PM then you need to be in your office by 8 AM. This is your time and there should be no one to give you suggestion and no one to interfere in what you do. From 9 AM onwards that time is your customer's time. Your time is either before 9 or after 6 PM.

So, when you reach at 8 AM your first job should be to sit and open your plan book or file. In this you should plan for the year, the month, the week and the day. As I discussed in an earlier chapter that you must divide your bigger goals (annual goals) in short term or day goals. I will give you an illustration on how to do it. This way you can do more things in a day. This way you can plan better and manage your things in an efficient way. If you divide your small goals in a week then you might miss on some things. However, if you plan your goals in the morning and analyze them in the evening then there are possibilities of more efficiency in work.

Following is a figure, just an example on how you can utilize your day:

10 AM	Meeting with the marketing person – discussion on advertisement on social media	
11 AM	Report on yesterday's customer inquiries	
12 PM	Follow up new customers – take their feedback	
1 PM	Meeting with staff – response of service or product	
2 PM	Setting goals with staff and brainstorming ideas	
3 PM	Read news – see market trend	
4 PM	See the product enhancement progress	
5 PM	Plans for tomorrow & complete anything that was left today	

This is a simple exercise that you must do in the morning. This will allow you to have a path for the whole day. You must have seen that I have empty columns on the right-hand side of the goals. Those are the boxes where you tick when you achieve a certain goal that you had set in the morning.

By this you will have a track of your activities for the whole day. Sometimes your day can be busy and there can be a couple of goals that remain unfulfilled. So, you just need to note them down and establish those goals the following day. When you make goals next day in the morning then you just need to write the left-over goals from the previous day along with the fresh goals.

This simple table can also be used to set weekly goals and monthly goals. You just need to replace the time column by days and dates for that. You can make your goals in a dairy or you can also use your mobile phone for that. I use my phone and just erase the goals as soon as I achieve them.

SALES RECORDS

There can be many businessmen who ignore this part sometimes and only concentrate on the quality of the product. That can be really dangerous. Some people think that sales will generally increase with time and take this part less seriously. You obviously need to concentrate on your product enhancement and quality, but the sales should also speak for itself.

If you keep ignoring the sales for a continuous period of time and do nothing, then you might fail in your business. sales records give you the exact picture of what you have achieved as a business and what have you earned from it.

Sales records are not the figures that needs to be reviewed every day. Instead you wait for the sales to happen and do the review monthly, quarterly, and then annually as well.

As a business you should never go down in your sales. If you do so, there is something very wrong. Even if your business is constant, still you are doing something wrong. Your sales as a business should always go up in terms of average profit and sales.

I will show you from a figure point of view. You must always make illustrations about your business, monthly, quarterly and annually. This will show you the actual position where you stand.

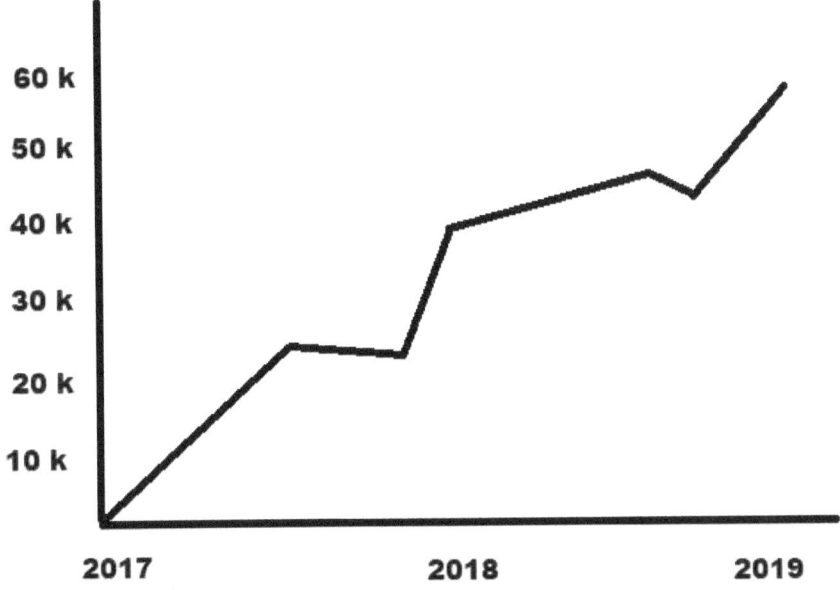

Figure - 1

In figure no. 1 you can clearly see that there were some ups and downs in the sales of the company between some months. But the average growth was always going up. That means every year there was better performance than the previous one which is a good sign for a business. There will be many ups and downs, but the average growth should not suffer. You might lose some business in November but if you work in the right direction then December can be great in terms of sales.

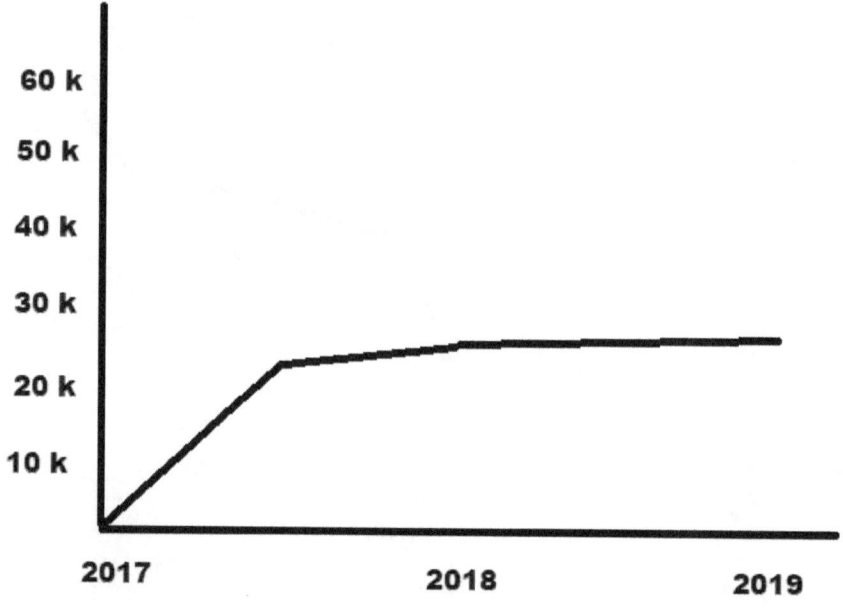

Figure - 2

In figure no. 2 it is very well seen that there was growth in the first year of the business but unfortunately the business failed to take off after 2018. There was no growth whatsoever. The sales and profits remained constant. This is not a good sign for a business. some might think that there is no loss in the business so there's no need to worry. But I and many business experts say that if the growth of business is constant then that means something is not right with your product or service or marketing. If you face this situation then you must always dig down deep and find out reasons for this situation.

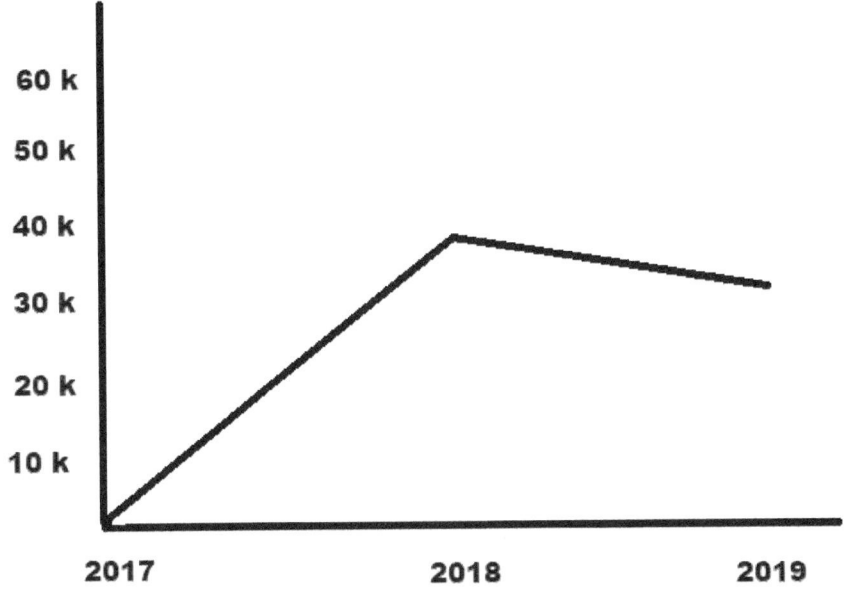

Figure - 3

It can be clearly analyzed from this image that the profit and sales went down after 2018. It is never a good sign for a new business. These days you can't think like 60's or 70's that a business needs some years to start giving you profits. No doubt that business takes time to give you profits but the drop of sales and profits after achieving them in previous year is a dangerous sign. This means that there is a discrepancy on your part be it in marketing, product or service. And something serious need to be done in order to change this trend.

ANNUAL REPORT

Annual report of a business should be evaluated by you after the completion of a year. This should contain all the details of your sales, profits, satisfied customers, complaints, product enhancement, expenses, successes, failures and each and everything that has happened in the past year.

This is a great way to learn about your business and yourself. I think that not only your business you must also make a parallel report about you for the past year. You must write a detailed report about yourself, about your achievements, anything that you were not able to achieve, anything that you would like to improve about yourself.

Business becomes a part of a person's life. In case of a job it is the office and colleagues that are dearer to you. But in the case of a business, your business is your friend and the one and only friend. **As a person you grow along with your business**. You learn so many things while doing business as you make so many sacrifices during that journey.

So, the annual report of you and your business should be studied by you in detail and take out positives out of that. Learn about yourself and about your business from that report. Try to make improvements in you and your business by using that annual report.

Annual report is like a score card that you used to get in schools. You will come to know about everything in detail. Try to improve your score card with each passing year.

ANNUAL GROWTH

I have already discussed about how an annual growth should look like using figures in the sales record chapter. The annual growth has two words in it. Annual and growth. So, it simply suggests that your business should grow year by year. It is suggested that there should be a growth of at least 15 -25 % every year to consider that you business is going well.

There can be times when there is no growth in the business, but no loss as well. In that situation you can recover from that if you make some extra efforts. I remember in the year 2015 I couldn't make more money than 2014. It was at par with the income in 2014. But if you consider the inflation rate then it means that your business should always grow by at least 20% because all the things around you get expensive by approximately 15-20 % every year.

That year I was disappointed, but I kept my cool and reviewed each and everything that I did in 2015. I made a detailed report about that and analyzed it in the December month of 2015. In that report I found many things that I did wrong. There were some things that worked in 2014 but the time keeps on changing. The way I was advertising my business had to change. I couldn't have found my errors if I had not kept record of everything. So always remember that you ought to keep detailed records of everything that you do and plan to do in your business.

That is when I introduced R & D in my business. I was never doing that before. By introducing R & D to my business I experimented with new things that were not done by me before. Experimentation might bring you failures but that is the part and parcel of R & D.

Once I started R & D, I found new ways of advertising my business and some new ways to develop products and services. I added a couple of other courses to my schedule and found tremendous results. I did a lot of enhancement in the courses that I offered. I went online through which I reached more customers.

This improvement only happened because I took notice of my annual growth and found flaws in it. I immediately worked on them and enhanced my business.

This happened with a combination of annual growth reports, annual sales records, R & D, product enhancement and annual reports of all sorts. These all things might look small but are essential for any kind of business. These things are universal and are not confined to only certain type of businesses.

If you apply these things in any aspect of life, then you can improve your life greatly. If you want to improve as a human being, then make your annual report. You will see the positive results in the next year. This system can be used in every aspect of life where improvement is required.

EXPENDITURE RECORD

This is another vital aspect of business. You must always keep a track of your expenditure. Make a file and keep all the bills, all the slips of even the smallest of items. This will tell you about the expenses that you do in your business and if there is a requirement for change.

You must go through your expenditure record every month to analyze your spending on all the items including minutest of things like tea/coffee. Knowingly or unknowingly there can be many things that you buy unnecessarily. When you have a written account of your expenditure then you must take out the things that you purchase unnecessarily and the things that are expensive. You must look for alternatives or simply avoid such things.

If you keep the expenditure low that means you are saving more for your business. You can utilize this money on advertisement or something more important.

So always keep an eye on your expenditure and make alterations where necessary.

OFTEN RENOVATE

Whether you have launched an application or a website; a shop or an office, it is of prime importance that you change the things quite often. You must renovate your business from time to time. You should make changes that are visible to your customers. The customers must realize that something new has been done or something better is on offer.

You must inculcate this attitude in your business as well as in your personal life. Renovation is always better than the previous setting. I renovate my office every 5 years. I completely change its outlook and interiors after every 5 years. I feel very fresh and my customers compliment on this too. Not only my office and classrooms, I also renovate the products and services that I provide. This also gives me a chance to increase the prices for my services and products.

I feel recharged and rejuvenated when I do the renovation. Recently I changed my office entirely and did expensive woodwork all around. These things are noticed by the customers. You will never see them appreciating a messy place, but they will surely praise about you and your office/premises to other people if the things are great. Renovating your business is also a part of advertisement.

For a businessperson every change is an opportunity to promote his/her business and products.

When I did renovation recently, I changed the hoardings, made a new website, redesigned the company's broacher, enhanced the logo's details and much more. So, the renovation was not limited to office, but it was holistic.

It is not about office. Many youngsters these days are earning millions from their online businesses. They only rely on their websites and online presence.

Thus, to apply this renovation system to your business you've got to see what are the things you need to renovate. If you take online classes, then you must buy a new camera. Your setup must be changed. If you have a restaurant then you must add a couple of new dishes to every cuisine that you serve. If you are a shop owner, then you must add on new products and change the display of the showroom. There ought to be visible changes to your business every 5 years. **Doing same things in the same way can worn you out**. You must apply these changes and renovate from time to time. This will not only give a change to customer but to your inner self as well.

SHOW OFF

As a businessperson you can never shy away from showing off yourself and your company. Even if you achieve a small thing professionally then show it off to everyone. Tell your family, friends and customers. Post your success on social media. Celebrate it with your staff members. Showing off is not a bad thing at all and neither it is a sign of arrogance. Showing off is important to let people know who you are and what you are achieving. You must never miss a chance to openly flaunt about your achievements and products. This greatly enhance your business.

Apart from this, your presence matters. You must be formally dressed in new and variety of clothing every day. You should have a set of more than 8 or 10 dresses. I generally wear coat and pant. It looks formal as well as authoritative. **You must look like a businessperson before becoming one**. Not a single part of you should look worn out. Your wristwatch should be glittering. Your shoes must be polished. Your mobile phone must be in tiptop condition.

Advertisement is another name for showing off. You show off about your company, products and services when you advertise. Similarly show off is important in every phase and part of business. As discussed in the earlier chapters, tell about yourself, what you do and what you make and whom you meet. Never miss a chance to show off your business to people. Always keep a handful of your visiting cards with you. Give it to anyone and everyone you meet. You've got to understand this simple thing that showing off will bring more business.

BEST ATTRACTS THE BEST

Always remember one thing in life that best attracts the best and you are the best. I have seen many people fail in life when they fail to deliver quality to their customers. There are businessmen who cater for people who prefer low quality products and services. They earn but they don't get quality customers. A business needs quality customer to grow its name and size.

So always remember that if you sell best quality things then you will get good quality customers. Good customers are always good for your business. When a customer buys a high-quality product or service then the customer will always flaunt it to others. This is how your brand name builds. On the other hand, if you are serving cheap products and services then your customers will not tell other people that they have bought your services.

It's a human nature and psychology. People only flaunt things that are expensive and rare. As a company you must keep your product rare and full of quality. This will give you advantages over your rivals. You can sell your products and services with better margins once it is established in the market. This is how you make your brand name. Make your customers say that xyz product is a bit expensive, but it is the best.

One of my friends is a baker and runs a famous bakery shop in the center of my hometown. Nowadays he's expanding to other parts of country as well. The reason he earned name and fame is that he remained unique and quality conscious. One of his famous products is artisan bread. Now a normal bread costs 30 bucks but his artisan bread costs around 150. A whopping five times higher than a normal bread would cost in the market.

People still buy it because it is unique and best in quality. As compared to the mass-produced bread his artisan bread is of supreme quality and customers who eat expensive and good quality products buy only his bread. By having uniqueness and supreme quality he was able to keep the margins high. Despite of selling at such a high price, he would sell more than 300 breads in a day. Even more than competitors who could only sell 150-200 of mass-produced bread.

So never think that if your product is expensive then it would have less sales. Just take an example of the leading smart phone manufacturing company. You know whom I am talking about. It is one of the most expensive mobile phones but still it is sold more than any other mobile of rival companies.

Be best and serve the best. You don't need to worry about the price of your product, once you establish your brand. Just focus on the quality and service. Your customers will make you famous by flaunting your brand to other people.

YOUR COMPETETION

Most people fail who try to compete with others. **You should always compete with only one person and that is you.** The reason I am saying this is that everyone has their own journey. You can't be like someone and no one can be like you. You need to be unique and different when you do business. You must think out of the box and out of the way if you want to be differentiated from the crowd.

There can be situations when you do same things as people do. But still you can do those things differently. You must find uniqueness in everything that you do when it comes to business. Everyone has their own story. If you try to follow others, then you lose your distinctiveness. Although using other people's ideas is not a bad thing but adding the spice of your own exclusivity is important.

You must be creative in your thought process. Always see whether you have improved or not from the previous week or month. See and analyze yourself on day 1 and then analyze yourself on day 30, then day 60, then day 90. The graph of improvement should always go up. This is what it means to compete with yourself. Becoming like others is not bad but you must carve a niche for yourself. Although I admire many personalities, but I never desire to be like one. I want to be like myself. You should have role models in life but should never make them your Gods.

When you are in the market you will have competition on all four sides. You must see it as a learning curve for yourself. Never feel intimidation from your competition. You can learn from them and add a bit of creativity to excel in your field.

Competition is a word that suppresses most people from starting a business. I have seen many people say that they don't want to start xyz business as there is already a lot of competition in it. As an average person you might say ok let's do something else. On the other hand, there are creative people who will think otherwise. They will say that there is a lot of competition in this field because there is great demand for this product or service.

Thinking like others can push you in a deep down well. You must have your own perspectives and opinions about decision making. You must be quick in your decision making and not waste time in deciding among options.

You should always try to focus on improving yourself from the past. This will also help you stay ahead of your competition. Improving yourself will also improve you among your competitors.

DON'T BE AFRAID TO FAIL

Most people are afraid of failure, that's why most people lead an average life. You must be a risk taker and not afraid to experiment in your business in order to be successful. There is no perfect guide or a book to succeed in a business. You must stick to the basics and try each and everything before you get a set formula. Formulas in business don't stay same for long. You need to tweak those formulas a bit, make improvements in that from time to time.

If you are afraid to fail, then you must never think of starting a business. Business is another name of taking risk. Why most people stick to a job is that they want to evade risk. I don't think that's wrong but if you think of becoming a great businessperson one day then taking risk is your path.

Many big businessmen have failed several times before becoming what they are today. I have seen many of my clients and friends fail before becoming the masters of their trades. As discussed earlier I had already told you that this book is not about making you the richest person in the world but the happiest one with good business stature and a person who is his own boss. This book is about motivating you to leave your 9 -5 job and do something dynamic and satisfying.

I am keen to give my personal example in this situation. I have always believed that you only learn when you fail. You never learn when you succeed. You keep on failing again and again and you will come to know about the things that are the cause of your failures. You've got to learn from those failures and try to achieve your goal again. You must keep on walking along your path and not worry about the failures.

There will be many people in your life who will remind you of your failure and try to give you opinions. These people will also include your parents, siblings, friends and spouse sometimes. You must ignore such people in life. You keep on listening to their opinions but do what you like and follow your dreams.

I have failed many times in my life. I wasn't great with my business knowledge, but I had one quality that my near and dear ones tell me. I was never afraid of taking risks in my life. I always tried new things despite failing again and again. I remember once in my life I had to take decision about changing my career, but my family was against that. I felt confused for the first time in my life, but my mother knew my plight and had these wonderful words for me:

She gave me words of wisdom that are stuck with me since then. I had made this my mantra of life. She told me "never be afraid of trying anything in life. Do what you like. Don't worry what others think about you. Just follow your path".

Although I was young at that time and had only been into my career for three years, but I had seen a lot of success and failure in that short period of time. Since then I have never looked back and don't give a damn about what others have to say about me. I just listen to me and do what my consciousness tells me to do.

PASSION WILL DEVELOP WITH MONEY

I might sound a bit contradictory to my views in this chapter, but this is the reality of life. Ultimately business means earning money. So, a good business is the one that generates good money. A great business is the one that generates great money. An average business is the one that generates average money. Business will always be judged by the money it earns.

Many people follow passion and are not worried about the income they generate. Some people succeed and some are left bankrupt. Business is a very complex game and the sooner you understand it the better it will be for you. There will be some phases of business in which you might think that I won't do it as it is not my passion. This is not the way businesses work. **Businesses are identified with the money it generates**. Passion has got little value in business. Sometimes your passion can take businesses to heights and sometimes it can be the cause of failure as well.

So, in some situations you must keep your passion differentiated from business. I have seen many people who keep on following their passions but miss on business opportunities. Once you start doing business your passion will develop with it. It doesn't matter whether you sell aero planes or cycles. You can earn millions and billions if you have the right intent for business and a good business model.

I am going to share a unique formula that I apply in my business life:

Life = Money and fame

It doesn't matter who you are, what you do, how you look, from where you belong, the eventual thing that everyone wants to acquire is money and fame in their lives. In this formula, on the left-hand side is the world, what you want to do(business/job), who you are, from where you are, basically everything in the world is on the left-hand side. The left-hand side is basically the present scenario. On the right side of the equals to is what you want and what you want to be or what you want to achieve. 95 % of people born on this planet wants to achieve what is on the right-hand side of equals to. On the left-hand side, it doesn't matter what you do and how you achieve it. Although you must be ethical in what you do.

So never stuck in your passion. You can pursue your passion while earning money as well. You will feel more passionate when you pursue your passions while earning good amount of money. Sometimes passion doesn't align with the business sense. So, it is better to keep your passion differentiated from your career.

Passion can make you a billionaire, but it can also be a cause of your failure in life.

OFTEN READ ABOUT SUCCESSFUL PEOPLE & MOTIVATION

I developed this habit a few years ago and since then I read about 50 books a year. I have a library of my own at my office and house. I enjoy reading books as much as I enjoy writing them. I wrote my first book after reading about 300 plus books. I wanted to learn the craft before I could start. Reading books can be really helpful in your business. As a businessperson you've got to be a frequent reader as abundance of knowledge will result in easy and better decision making.

If you don't like reading books or novels in particular, then I suggest reading about famous personalities or motivation. By reading about them you will get an insight about their lives and their childhood. You will see that most of the people started from scratch. By most I mean 95% or more. I started reading books about 8 years back and the first one that I picked was 'The long walk to freedom' by Nelson Mandela. It was very inspiring and whenever I face difficulties in my life then I get a lot of help from that book. Reading auto biographies is like listening to that person personally. When you read these sorts of books, you get tremendous amount of encouragement in all facets of life. I am going to share a list of few life changing books that I have read:

1. The long walk to freedom – Nelson Mandela
2. My experiments with truth – Mahatma Gandhi
3. The magic of thinking big – David J Schwartz
4. The autobiography – Benjamin Franklin
5. Biographies and autobiographies of Steve Jobs, Dhiru Bhai Ambani and Barack Obama

There can be endless number of books that can inspire you. You must read for at least 1 hour every day. This will not only increase your knowledge but will also make you a better person. It will give you time to think about you as a person. These people have inspired millions of people all over the world. Their words have the power to change anyone's mind.

VISUALIZE SUCCESS

Visualization is something that very few people can have in life. Visualizing anything is just preparing your mind for the future. Visualization is a mere prediction of how the things will unfold in future. You must be good at visualizing success in your business. This is not a skill that can be learnt. Many people fail to learn this in their whole life. There are very few things in life that comes naturally. I think that the skill of visualization is inbuilt, and people often succeed who have this skill in them.

I can tell you one exercise that can help you visualize success. You remember that how I showed you about planning the day according to time in a table. Similarly, you can visualize success using that timetable. You must draw a timetable month and year wise. Then write the amount of money you want to earn in that month or year. Then work your way up according to that. This will give you a benchmark of success. This will force you in achieving your targets. This will act as a milestone that you look to achieve in your journey. This is how a success visualization table should look like:

2020	2021	2022	2023	2024
200,000	300,000	500,000	700,000	1 million

This simple table will help you to make plans for the future and push you to your limits. Visualizing is very important in business.

BE PATIENT

Patience is the key to success. **Being patient is one of the biggest qualities of a businessperson**. Lack of patience closes many businesses when they are not far from being successful. As I told you earlier that passion should not be mixed with business. But one thing that a businessperson should be passionate about is the passion to do business. This passion will also bring patience. If you have patience, then you will give your business more time to respond. Some businesses shoot up sooner than other businesses. It entirely depends on the business type.

Along with being patient you must be proactive as well. Being too patient can also be fatal for a business. You must know when to make changes in your business in order to get more response.

For an example, if you are trying a new method of advertisement. You must give it at least 60 days before you start seeing the results. You must not continuously change your methods in business. This will disrupt the chain and will not reap you any benefits. You should not be desperate to churn out results from nothing. You must be practical in your approach and wait for the right time. Timing is everything in business.

Once you have applied all these methods and have visualized your success then the success will definitely come to you. You just need to be a bit patient.